Getting Dressed

Sheila Jackson and Tim Wood

Photographs by Maggie Murray
Illustrations by Sheila Jackson

Contents

A & C Black · London

What do you wear?

How long does it take you to get dressed in the morning? You can probably throw on your clothes, do up a zip and a few buttons, and you're ready in only a few minutes. Your garments, even the school clothes you wear for much of the year, are light, comfortable and practical. When you go shopping for clothes you can find a wide range of fashionable items in dozens of different clothes shops.

At the turn of the century, when your great grandparents were children, getting dressed took much longer. Clothes in those days were not very comfortable, and putting them on could take a long time. Sometimes two people were needed to wrestle with the complicated fastenings.

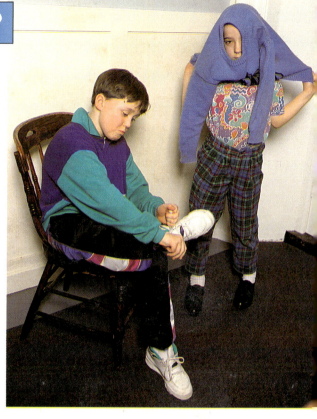

▲ Modern clothes are simple to put on and comfortable to wear. Many of them are made of artificial fibres or other materials which are easy to keep clean and neat.

Schoolchildren in 1907. At the turn of the century, clothes were difficult to keep clean and could be very uncomfortable.

Many clothes were made from heavy materials which were hard to keep clean. Garments were often expensive to buy and there were few clothes shops. Lots of people had to wear second-hand clothes or hand-me-downs, or make their own clothes. Rich people had their clothes specially made for them.

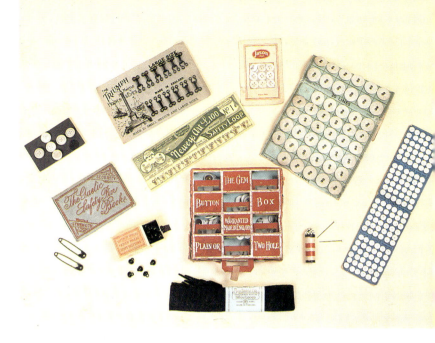

▲ Here is a selection of Edwardian fastenings. At the turn of the century convenient modern fastenings, such as zips and Velcro, had not been invented. Many of the fastenings had to be removed when clothes were washed, to stop them being crushed in the mangle. They were sewn back on after the clothes had been ironed.

◀ This boy tried on a Norfolk suit at the Geffrye Museum. He found it terribly hot and prickly to wear. Your great grandpa probably wore a suit like this almost every day.

Time-line

	Great great grandparents were born			Great grandparents were born		
	pre-1880s	**1880s**	**1890s**	**1900s**	**1910s**	**1920s**
Important events	**1876** Alexander Graham Bell invents telephone	**1888** Dunlop invents pneumatic tyre	**1890** Moving pictures start **1896** First modern Olympic Games	**1901** Queen Victoria dies. Edward VII becomes King **1903** Wright brothers fly first plane	**1910** George V becomes King **1914–18** World War I	**1926** General Strike in Britain
Clothing dates	**1850** Jeans made by Levi Strauss in the USA. They were designed as hard-wearing trousers for miners **1851** The first sewing machine for use in the home invented in the USA by Merritt Singer **1865** The first rubber wellington boots made in Edinburgh **1866** The first dry cleaner in Britain opens in Perth	Dinner jackets first appear **1883** The first artificial fibre (artificial silk) made for use in lightbulbs **1887** Knicker elastic introduced to Britain **1889** The first electric sewing machine produced in the USA **1889** Rubber soles and heels first fitted to shoes and boots	Feathers very popular for boas and for hat decoration **1892** The first gymslip worn at the Hampstead Physical Training College **1893** The zip invented in the USA **1898** The first artificial yarn (viscose) suitable for dyeing and weaving, made from wood pulp	Enormous hats become fashionable for ladies **1900** The first old school tie introduced for old Etonians **1902** Khaki uniforms worn throughout the British Army **1907** The first household detergent (Persil) manufactured **1909** The first bra advertised in *Vogue* magazine	Narrow 'hobble skirts' make walking difficult for the wearers **1910** The first rayon stockings made in Germany ● After 1914 there are fewer servants to look after clothes. Women begin to demand clothes for themselves and their children which are more sensible and which can be cleaned more easily	Trouser suits for women, called beach pyjamas are introduced, skirts become much shorter and short hair becomes fashionable for women ● Russian Ballet costumes influence dress. Russian boots become fashionable

4

This time-line shows some of the important events since your great great grandparents were children, and some of the events and inventions which have changed clothing styles and fabrics, the ways in which clothes are made, and shopping for clothes.

andparents were born		**Parents were born**		**You were born**		
930s	1940s	1950s	1960s	1970s	1980s	1990s

930s	1940s	1950s	1960s	1970s	1980s	1990s
Edward abdicates. rge VI omes King. irst vision dcasts World II starts	**1941** Penicillin successfully tested **1945** World War II ends **1947** First supersonic plane	**1952** Elizabeth II becomes Queen	**1961** Yuri Gargarin first man in space **1969** Neil Armstrong first man on the moon	**1973** Britain enters the Common Market	**1981** First successful space shuttle flight	

930s	1940s	1950s	1960s	1970s	1980s	1990s
sers me pted wear omen The first es made seproof c on sale een ett mes the woman in in to wear s shorts The first er zip Nylon first	During the war years clothing is rationed and simple garments, called Utility Clothing, are on sale ● Most people wear some kind of uniform ● Women's hats replaced by headscarves and turbans **1946** The first British nylon stockings go on sale ● Men's 'Y front' underpants invented	Increased use of artificial fibres ● Ponytail hairstyles popular ● Pointed 'Winkle Picker' shoes fashionable for men. High, pointed stiletto heels fashionable for women ● Padded bras and layers of petticoats worn by younger women ● Tight denim jeans fashionable **1951** Terylene garments go on sale	Mini skirts, 'hot pants' and platform shoes fashionable for women ● Flared trousers fashionable for men ● Brighter colours become popular ● Light girdles and roll-ons become more fashionable as women rely more on diet and exercise rather than corsets to keep them slim ● Tights replace stockings **1967** Fashion designer Paco Rabanne makes a dress from plastic discs linked by chains	Practical clothes such as jeans, dungarees and T-shirts become popular ● Skinhead and punk rocker outfits with outrageous spiky hairstyles become fashionable ● Laura Ashley clothes become popular **1971** 'Maxi' coats and dresses become fashionable	Increase in protests against fur used as clothing ● Anoraks become popular	Sportswear, such as trainers and shell suits, becomes fashionable for everyday wear ● Leatherwear becomes popular

5

Layer upon layer

How many layers of clothes do you put on in the morning? Your great grandma probably put on at least five layers, and possibly many more in cold weather.

People at the turn of the century were great believers in keeping their limbs warm. Houses were not as easy to heat as they are today, so people kept warm by making sure that their underwear covered everything. Men and boys dressed in long-sleeved vests and long underpants made of wool, flannel, cotton or silk.

Mr Pym, who was about your age in 1910, remembers:

'We wore flannel pants and vests in winter, and cotton ones in summer'.

▼ Underwear like this was worn by girls of your age in Edwardian times. Some vests and knickers could be buttoned together to make single garments.

▲ These girls tried on some Victorian underwear at the Nottingham Museum of Costume. The girl on the right wears a flannel petticoat which she found hot and heavy. The girl on the left wears a pair of Victorian drawers. She was amazed to find that they had a huge gap down the middle because the two legs were not sewn together. Can you think why they were made like this?

◄ Vests and pants for men and boys were sometimes worn separately, but were often sold in one suit of underwear, called combinations. The pants either buttoned or tied with tapes at the front, so they were easy to undo.

► Your great grandma wore a liberty bodice like this when she was your age. It was made of cotton in summer or fleecy material in winter.

▲ Pink silk underwear for men. The pants fastened with tapes at the front.

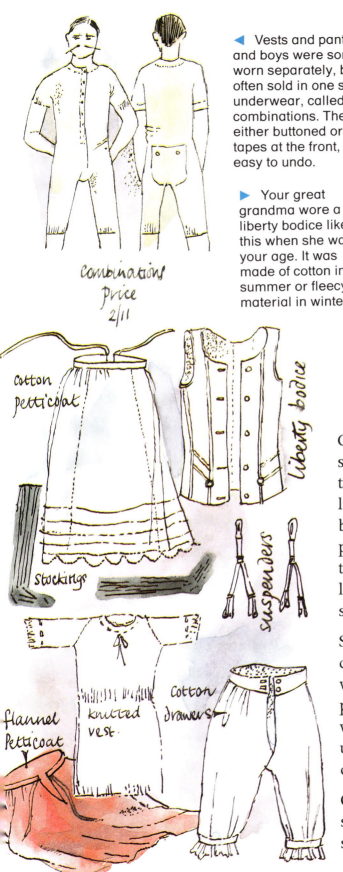

combinations
Price
2/11

cotton petticoat

liberty bodice

Stockings

suspenders

flannel Petticoat

knitted vest

cotton drawers

Girls wore vests which could have short or long sleeves. Over the vests they wore either liberty bodices or lightly boned corsets called camisole bodices. Most girls wore at least one pair of drawers, and a second, thicker pair in winter, as well as at least two petticoats made of cotton or silk, or flannel in winter.

Some mothers even sewed their children into their underwear for the winter by stitching the vest and pants together while the child was wearing them. The only washing the underwear received was when the child took a bath.

Children wore woollen or cotton stockings, held up with garters or suspenders, and lace-up boots.

Unhealthy clothes

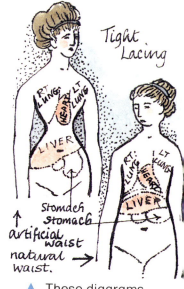

In Victorian times, women wore corsets and petticoats made of cotton or flannel over their lower layers of underwear. On top of these they wore heavy woollen or velveteen outer clothing.

During the Edwardian period some doctors realised that these layers of heavy, tight clothing were not healthy. A few women, especially those who wanted to lead more active lives, joined a movement for 'Rational Dress', to encourage the wearing of practical, comfortable clothes.

Some of the reformers' ideas were very strange. Some doctors thought tightly-buckled belts caused kidney disease, and advised men to wear braces instead. Tight collars were thought to make the head too hot, while open-neck shirts were thought to cause exposure, pneumonia and premature death!

▲ These diagrams in a magazine of about 1900 showed the way in which tight corsets could deform the rib cage and damage the inner organs. Wearing a corset, a woman's waist could measure as little as 50 cm. Compare this to the size of your mother's waist.

▼ In spite of doctors' advice many women wore corsets like this one up until the 1920s. Whalebones or metal struts in the corset shaped the figure, but restricted heart and lung movement. Corsets made normal breathing impossible and stopped the proper circulation of the blood.

Other ideas were more sensible. Tightly-laced corsets were blamed for deforming women by crushing the ribs and squashing the heart and liver. Some doctors believed that the weight of women's dresses and the many layers they wore caused parts of the body to become overheated. The reformers recommended that:

▲ Edwardian girls were much more comfortably dressed than their mothers. They often wore loose, light dresses such as the one this girl tried on at the Geffrye Museum. Notice that the weight of the dress is taken on the shoulders rather than on the hips.

First, the vital organs situated in central regions of the body must be allowed free movement.

Second, a uniform temperature of the body must be preserved.

Third, weight of clothing must be reduced to a minimum.

Fourth, the shoulders, and not the hips, must serve as the base of support.

Some ideas put forward by the clothing reformers did influence fashions for girls, and led to them wearing fewer layers of lighter, more comfortable clothes during the Edwardian period. But the reformers' advice was largely ignored by women, who continued to wear restricting and dangerous corsets under many layers of uncomfortable, heavy outer clothing until the 1920s.

◄ A suffragette demonstration. Even many suffragettes, who wanted more equality for women, still wore corsets and tight belts. But the girls are wearing much looser clothes.

School uniform

You probably spend a lot of your time in your school clothes. What would your great grandparents have worn at your age? It is quite possible that they may not have gone to school much. Although the 1870 Education Act made school compulsory for children under 13, many pupils from poor homes went absent from school to do odd-jobs to help support their families. In country areas children worked in the fields, especially at harvest time.

Schoolchildren at the turn of the century. They do not wear uniform, but they have very similar clothing. Notice the great number of hats and caps.

Most children did not usually have school uniforms, but they were expected to wear sensible clothes which looked neat and tidy when they were at school.

Boys and girls wore stout leather boots which laced up the front, woollen or cotton stockings, and school ties. Girls usually wore pinafores over their dresses. Boys often wore knickerbocker suits and stiff collars.

◀ Rich children who went to public schools were fully equipped with smart uniforms. These boys were pupils at Eton.

▶ Girls could not play games very easily in their normal clothes. The layers of flannel petticoats were too hot and awkward for sports such as hockey or cricket. By 1900, girls began to dress in more practical, lighter gymslips. On their feet, they wore rubber-soled gym shoes if their parents could afford them.

▼ This Edwardian advertisement shows one type of games kit worn by girls who played games at school.

Children from very poor homes might go to school dressed in rags, wearing nothing at all on their feet. But almost everyone, however rich or poor, wore a hat. Girls wore straw hats in the summer, and felt hats in winter. Boys wore caps or top hats, and some wore straw boaters in summer.

Harry Redman, who is 81, remembers:

'We had no school uniform, but we all wore caps. We had to raise them to any ladies we met and to the vicar.'

For games boys wore knee-length shorts and long-sleeved shirts made of stout cotton. Many girls wore their ordinary school clothes for games.

11

Working clothes

Can you tell what a person's job is just by looking at what he or she is wearing? At the turn of the century, it was possible to make quite an accurate guess about someone's job by looking at their clothes.

Businessmen, undertakers, cab drivers, male shop-assistants and clerks wore dark suits and top hats. Tradespeople, skilled workers and some servants wore bowler hats. Farmers and other country workers wore practical, less formal clothing.

▲ One of the girls tried on some leather gaiters. They were much too big. She also found them awkward to lace. Harry Redman told her that he had found gaiters very warm and practical for his work.

fireman
dustman
train guard
clerk
pageboy
shepherd

Harry Redman, who left school at the age of 12 to work on the land, remembers:

'I put on my first pair of long trousers when I started work on the farm. But most of the time I wore knee breeches and leather gaiters.'

Some farmworkers wore smocks, others protected their clothes with aprons. Harry Redman and Mr Pym, who also worked on a farm, remember:

'We always wore old clothes for work with hobnail boots. If we were doing anything dirty, we wore aprons made from old sacks.'

Many shopkeepers, especially butchers and fishmongers, wore aprons and straw boaters. The hundreds of thousands of servants employed by rich families at the time were easy to identify. Each had his or her distinctive uniform.

▲ Almost everyone at the turn of the century wore lace-up boots. Shoes became more popular after 1910. Some workers, especially those in the north, wore clogs with leather uppers and wooden soles. This boy tried on a pair and discovered that each sole was shod with iron, just like a horse shoe. This made the clogs very heavy.

Workers, such as builders, miners and dustmen, wore rough clothes and heavy boots or clogs.

Round leather hats with long flaps which hung down the wearer's back were popular among workers who had to carry heavy loads. The flap protected the worker's neck. Other workers wore flat caps. Almost all workers wore shirts without collars.

Clothes for fun

Do you play any sports? Do you wear special clothes while you play? One hundred and fifty years ago, people did not play sports much. But after 1870 there was a huge growth in sporting activity for men and women.

▶ Young Edwardian boys were often dressed in sailor suits. These became fashionable when the Prince of Wales went into the Royal Navy.

Most of the visitors to the seaside in Edwardian times wore their ordinary clothes on the beach.

▶ Roller skating was a very popular sport. Some women even played football wearing roller skates.

The rich went motoring, yachting, riding, hunting, shooting and fishing. The middle classes enjoyed tennis, croquet, archery and golf in the summer, and skating in the winter. One of the fastest-growing sports was cycling. And the boom in seaside holidays, caused by rising wages and the development of railways, led to more people swimming and walking.

One reason for the increased interest in sport was that, after 1870, people had more paid holidays. Another was that doctors began to advise people to exercise for their health. As a result, more sport was played at school. For the first time girls were encouraged to play sports such as hockey, and to do physical training at school.

Each sport needed a special outfit and it was important to wear the 'correct' dress. Today these outfits seem restricting and heavy, but at the time they were much looser and more comfortable than ordinary clothes.

▲ Edwardian lady cyclists found their long skirts could become entangled in the bicycle chain. This girl tried out one of the Edwardian skirt lifters which were used by lady cyclists. A clip holds the hem of the dress. The cord is pulled tight and fastened to the waistband, hitching up the hem of the dress.

Clothes for church

◀ Churchgoers in their 'Sunday best', attending a christening in 1887. Women wore their best outfits, usually crowned with a bonnet or spectacular hat. Men wore dark suits or tail coats with stiff collars.

▼ A selection of Edwardian collars. These were stiffened with starch and attached to the shirt with front and back studs. The shirt front was fastened with shirt studs, and the cuffs with cufflinks.

Many more people went to church at the turn of the century than do today. Going to church was an important duty for the rich and the middle classes. Their servants were expected to attend the services as well. Many working class families who lived in the country also went to church, although churchgoing was less common among workers in towns.

Churchgoers made a special effort to look smart, by putting on their 'Sunday best'. Mr Pym, who was born in 1893, remembers:

▲ This boy tried on a stiff collar. It wasn't very comfortable. The edge of the collar cut into his neck and the stud dug into his throat.

'We only wore our best clothes on Sunday to go to church and then Sunday School. We weren't allowed to romp around in them and had to take them off to play afterwards.'

One sad reason for people going to church was to attend a funeral. After a death, the close relatives of the person who had died went into mourning. 'Full' mourning could last at least a year. Women wore only black clothes and black jewellery made from jet during this period. Men wore black armbands, hatbands and ties. Even the children were expected to wear black ties and black armbands or sashes.

Many mourning clothes and bands were made of black crêpe, which had a crinkly texture. This material became associated with death and it was thought unlucky to have black crêpe in the house unless someone was in mourning.

After the period of 'full' mourning was over, a woman often went into 'half' mourning. She wore only dark clothes – grey, purple and mauve were considered to be suitable colours.

▶ This girl tried on a Victorian mourning cape and bonnet. She found the cape very heavy. The boy is wearing the sort of armband an Edwardian boy of his age would have worn while in mourning.

Children from rich homes wore lots of winter clothes to keep them warm. Mary Sherman–James remembers the advice her nurse used to give her over 75 years ago:

'She always told us to wrap up warmly in cold weather. I always wore a woolly muffler and gloves.'

She went on to describe a favourite aunt:

'She always wore a fur muff in which she hid biscuits to give to the children.'

▲ In Victorian and Edwardian times, button boots were sometimes worn instead of lace-ups. These girls learned how to do up the buttons using button hooks. They were surprised how easily the hook pulled the buttons through the holes.

► This child tried on an Edwardian fur cape and muff. She thought it was cruel that animal skins were used to make clothes in 1900. What do you think about this?

Wrapping up warmly meant wearing an overcoat, woollen stockings, a hat, a big scarf, and gloves or a muff. In wet weather children put big rubber shoes, called galoshes, over their ordinary shoes to keep their feet dry.

Girls and women often wore shawls which could be put over the head in bad weather.

COMPLETE OUTFITS

'Eton'

'Royal'

▲ The children examined an Edwardian hat made of a whole stuffed pheasant. They thought it was cruel to use birds as hat decorations. Ladies who wore hats like these were advised not to go into the country during the shooting season!

▼ Children wore gaiters in cold weather. A hook was used to fasten all the buttons up the side of each gaiter.

▲ Winter coats like these could be found in clothing catalogues at the turn of the century. The bulge on the girl's bottom was caused by a cloth pad which was strapped to her waist. These pads, called bustles, were no longer fashionable by 1910.

Children from poor homes were expected to go out to work. Their parents could not afford to buy them warm winter clothes. Mr Pym, who left school and started work on a farm in 1909, remembers:

'We worked so hard that we didn't feel the cold in winter. I never wore coats, gloves or even scarves. I did put on Wellington boots when it was muddy though.'

Party clothes

What would you wear for a party? At the turn of the century, only children from well-off homes went to parties. They ate party food, such as jellies and cakes. They played party games, such as blind man's buff, flip the kipper and hide-and-seek. There was often an entertainer, and conjurers were specially popular.

◄ Edwardian children at a party.

Girls' party dresses were mostly pale colours. Perhaps this was because pale shades are difficult to keep clean and so dresses made in these colours were obviously special. Other outfits were made of dark velvet. Many dresses were trimmed with lace and ribbon and some had wide, brightly-coloured sashes.

The young partygoer usually wore white shoes made of satin or soft leather. Each shoe was fastened with a pearl button. Silk stockings, which were either white or the same colour as the dress, and matching hair ribbons completed the outfit.

On their way to and from a party, girls usually wore party cloaks. These were often made of red velvet and trimmed with white fur. If the weather was chilly, the wearer could pull the hood up to keep out the wind.

Younger boys often wore satin suits with trousers or breeches. Fancy dress was also popular. Older boys wore jackets, waistcoats and knickerbockers. Shirts, which were often made of silk, usually had deep, soft collars. Brightly-coloured shirt studs were a popular way of decorating the shirt front.

▲ The girls examined some Edwardian party dresses at the Nottingham Museum of Costume. They found that the dresses were lavishly decorated with hand-made lace.

► Fans similar to this one, which is made from ivory, were carried by girls from rich families at parties in Edwardian times.

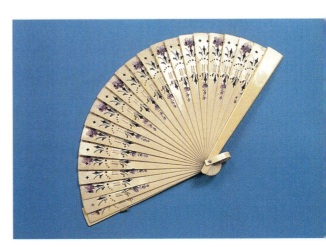

A new outfit

Have you ever looked at the labels in your clothes to see where the clothes come from? Most of your clothes are made in factories, many of which are in other countries. The clothes are sent 'ready to wear' from the factories to be sold in high-street shops. When you buy clothes, you probably try on several garments in different sizes and choose the one which fits you best.

In 1900, there were fewer clothes shops than there are today, and not many of them sold ready-made clothes. Some of the new department stores, such as Gamages which opened in 1878, sold clothes which could be bought 'off the peg'. But these stores were found mainly in large cities, and the clothes were expensive.

The customer chose cloth and trimmings from a haberdashers shop. She took the cloth and the trimmings to to the dressmaker where she was measured.

Buying fashionable clothes could be time-consuming. Customers were usually given refreshments while the shop assistants modelled the garments. A copy of the chosen gown was then made to fit the customer.

Some dressmakers worked at home using the kitchen or dining room table after meals had been cleared away.

From 1900 onwards, more factories turned to producing off-the-peg clothing. But, for many years, the large department store remained the place to buy clothes. It was not until after 1945 that small shops selling ready-made clothes began to appear in large numbers.

At the turn of the century, people from the upper and middle classes had most of their clothes made for them. Men went to tailors, hatters and cobblers to have outfits and footwear made to their own measurements. Women bought the cloth and trimmings and then went to a dressmaker to have the clothes made for them.

◀ Having an outfit made.

Harrods Stores. No 18 Department

Youth's Clothing First Floor

boots &
shoes

Many people had either no time or not enough money to visit a high-class dressmaker, tailor or department store. Some, especially those who lived in the country, relied on local seamstresses. Mary Sherman–James, who lived in a small village during her childhood over 70 years ago, remembers:

'There was a woman in the village who made all our new dresses. She made her own patterns which she copied from magazines.'

Local dressmakers made their patterns in brown paper or newspaper, and usually owned a tailor's dummy. Customers sometimes bought their own patterns from drapers' shops.

Some large stores sold clothes by mail order, so that people who lived in the country could send away for them. Customers usually paid cash on delivery. By 1900, mail order shopping had become popular with the middle classes and with better-off workers.

One of the most popular catalogues came from Gamages. It contained a huge range of goods, including clothing. The store was the official outfitter for the Boy Scout movement and also offered a large choice of camping gear and explorers' equipment. Many parents bought their children's school uniforms from the catalogue.

▲ ▶ Boys' clothing in a mail order catalogue of about 1900, some of it suitable for school wear. Mail order shopping was very convenient, especially for those who lived in remote areas.

Norfolk · Cape coat · Jack Tar

overcoats · caps · ties · hose · shoes · towels · SAMUELS Bros.

▶ An Edwardian hand-operated sewing machine. The sewing machine was originally invented in 1790. The first small machine suitable for home use was invented in 1851 by the American, Merritt Singer.

The magazine from which the pattern came.

▲ Some Edwardian women's magazines contained dress patterns. These children tried one out. They were amazed by the amount of cloth needed to make a single dress.

But many people, especially those who were not well-off, made their own garments. In many families mothers, daughters, grandmothers and aunts made or knitted clothes. Some people sewed their garments by hand, but by 1890 portable sewing machines had become quite common and were used in many homes.

◄ A second-hand clothes shop at the turn of the century. Poor families went to shops like this, or to clothes pedlars, to buy good-quality garments at prices they could afford.

Making clothes last

Your parents probably complain about how quickly you grow out of your clothes. Parents no doubt made similar complaints a hundred years ago. But the clothes bought or made for your great grandparents were almost always a size too big, to allow for growth. Shoes were often bought too large as well, and the toes stuffed with cotton wool until the child grew into them.

When clothes became too small for the child, they were passed on to another member of the family as 'hand-me-downs'. Sometimes, even in rich homes, the same item of clothing would be worn by several children, one after the other, over a period of years.

▼ This child tried her hand at mending clothes, using items which are over 90 years old. You can see a sewing basket on the right, and a large card of buttons and two darning mushrooms in the foreground.

Mary Sherman—James, who is 87, remembers:

'We wore hand-me-downs for ordinary clothes. Our cousins were older than we were and passed on their old things to us.'

◄ Your great grandma probably wore a dress like this one from the Geffrye Museum. A cotton pinafore, which could easily be washed, was worn on top to protect the dress. The 'growth tucks' round the hem of the dress were let down as the child grew.

People took great care of their clothes, to try to make them last as long as possible. Outer garments made of materials such as wool or silk were hard to wash. Those garments were brushed, sponged or steamed to refresh them, then hung up in the wardrobe. Evil-smelling mothballs were hung beside them to protect the fabric from insects.

Rich people sent clothes to laundries to be cleaned or mended, or had them laundered at home by their maids. In poorer households, mothers, elder daughters and maiden aunts washed, cleaned and repaired clothes themselves.

Harry Redman, born in 1910, remembers:

'My mother used to sew something every night. I've still got the wooden darning mushroom she used to darn our socks. They always seemed to go through at the toes and heels first.'

▲ Norfolk jackets, like this one from the Geffrye Museum, were very popular garments for boys at the turn of the century. The pleats in the back left room for growth and allowed the boy to move his arms freely and easily.

▲ Edwardian clothes cleaning equipment. The ball is made of a substance called Fuller's earth. This was put on as a paste then brushed off when dry. The large brush is for clothes and the smaller one for hats.

▼ Clothes brushes at the turn of the century included curved hat brushes and stiff brushes for reviving the pile on velveteen clothes. This boy tried out a curved hat brush on a silk top hat.

Growing up

When your great grandparents began to grow up, they wore more adult clothes and were expected to behave like adults.

Middle-class and upper-class boys were expected to wear suits and stiff collars all the time. Collars were often made of starched cotton. Cheaper ones were made of cardboard. Some were made of a new material called celluloid, a kind of early plastic which was very flammable. Harry Redman, who was born in 1910, remembers:

'A lad I knew had scars round his neck where his celluloid collar caught fire from the flame of a candle.'

Middle-class and upper-class girls over the age of 16 were no longer allowed to let their hair hang down loosely or in plaits. They had to 'put it up' in elaborate hairstyles on top of their heads. In spite of the warnings of the clothing reformers, many young women were expected to wear corsets, although after 1910 these were less severely boned.

▲ Young adults from rich families spent a life of luxurious leisure. Their hardest work was getting dressed for an evening out at the theatre, a smart dinner party or a glamorous ball. This drawing, done in 1890, shows a young girl at her first ball. You can tell from the narrowness of her waist that she is wearing a corset.

◄ This boy learned how to tie a bow tie. Rich Victorian and Edwardian gentlemen wore bow ties with evening dress at theatres, balls and banquets.

Most middle-class girls stayed with their families until they got married, sewing and embroidering their own clothes. Some of these women started careers, such as teaching, nursing or working in shops.

Young adults from poorer families had much less money and less time to enjoy themselves. Many boys started work at the age of 13. They wore whatever clothes were thought suitable for their jobs. They dressed in their best clothes to visit a music hall or a fair for an occasional treat.

Working-class girls usually became servants or factory workers. Girls who went into service needed at least two working dresses and aprons. Their parents often struggled to provide even these few garments.

▲ This is just a small selection of the equipment a young Edwardian lady needed: 1 Hat pins to keep on hats in windy weather. 2 Hair combs to keep elaborate hairstyles in place. 3 Feathers to decorate the hair. 4 A matching collection containing hat pins, a belt buckle, and studs to fasten a blouse.

▼ This Edwardian opera hat folded flat so it could be kept under the theatre seat during the performance.

How to find out more

Start here	To find out about...	Who will have...
Old people	What people wore at the turn of the century	Old photos, scrap books, memories, souvenirs
Museums	Old things to look at and possibly handle	Reconstructed rooms and displays of objects connected with clothes
Libraries	● Loan collections ● Reference collections ● Information to help your research ● Local history section	● Books to borrow ● Magazines, especially *Punch, Graphic, Illustrated London News* ● Useful addresses, guidebooks, additional reference material ● Newspapers and guides to look at; photographs of local people; tape recordings of old people remembering what they wore
Manufacturers of products connected with clothes	History of their products	Booklets, pictures, advertisements and information about the history of their products
Junk shops Old clothes shops	What people bought Old clothes	Old magazines showing clothes Old clothes and accessories
Local history society	Your area a hundred years ago	Information, reference material, and advice on how to further your research

Who can tell you more?

They can. Use a tape recorder for recording their memories. Handle anything they show you with great care and if they lend you something, label it with their name and keep it somewhere safe.

The curator or the museum's education officer. Many museums have bookshops and a notice board where you can look for further information

- The librarian
- The reference librarian
- Ask the archivist for the name and address of the local history society

The Public Relations Officer of the company, part of whose job is to help with queries like yours

The owner. Specialist shopkeepers are very enthusiastic and knowledgeable about their stock. They may know of local people with collections of things connected with clothing. They may be able to give you further contacts and addresses

The secretary

Places to visit

There are too many costume museums in the UK for us to include a comprehensive list in the space available. Refer to the *Cambridge Guide to the Museums of Britain and Ireland* by Hudson and Nicholls (CUP) for a full list. Most local museums have sections dedicated to costume. The following places have particularly good or relevant displays, reconstructions or exhibitions connected with clothes and costume which are known to us:

Beccles and District Museum, Newgate, Beccles, Suffolk NR34 9QA. Tel: 0502 712628
Bethnall Green Museum of Childhood, Cambridge Heath Road, London E2 9PA. Tel: 081 980 3204
Bexhill Manor Costume Museum, Manor House Gardens, Old Town, Bexhill-on-Sea, East Sussex TN40 2JA
Brighton Art Gallery and Museum, Church Street, Brighton, East Sussex BN1 1UE. Tel 0273 603005
The Cecil Higgins Museum and Art Gallery, Castle Close, Bedford, Bedfordshire MK40 3NY. Tel: 0234 211222
The Gallery of English Costume, Platt Hall, Platt Fields, Rusholme, Manchester M14 5LL. Tel: 061 224 5217
The Geffrye Museum, Kingsland Road, London E2 8EA. Tel: 071 739 8368/9893
Imperial War Museum, Lambeth Road, London SE1 6HZ. Tel: 071 735 8922
Hoar Cross Hall, Hoar Cross, Nr Burton-upon-Trent, Staffordshire DE13 8QS. Tel: 028375 224
The Museum of Costume, Assembly Rooms, Bennett Street, Bath, Avon BA1 2QH. Tel: 0225 61111
The Museum of Costume and Textiles, 43–51 Castle Gate, Nottingham NG1 6AF. Tel: 0602 411881
Presteigne and District Museum, Shire Hall, Presteigne, Powys
Shambellie House Museum of Costume, New Abbey, Nr Dumfries, Dumfriesshire. Tel: 038785 375
Sudbury Hall Museum of Childhood, Sudbury Hall, Sudbury, Derbyshire DE6 5HT. Tel: 028378 305
York Castle Museum, York YO1 1RY. Tel: 0904 53611

Useful addresses

The Friends of Fashion, c/o Museum of London, London Wall, London EC2Y 5HN. Tel: 071 600 3699
Phone for details on Tuesdays or Thursdays between 11 a.m. and 2 p.m.
The Geffrye Museum, Kingsland Road, London E2 8EA. Tel: 071 739 8368/9893. This is one of the few places where children can actually try on clothes. Ring for details.

Index

Published by A & C Black (Publishers) Limited
35 Bedford Row
London WC1R 4JH
© 1992 A & C Black (Publishers) Ltd

ISBN 0–7136–3634–3

A CIP catalogue record for this book is available from the British Library.

Filmset by August Filmsetting, Haydock, St Helens

Printed in Italy by L.E.G.O.

Acknowledgements

The author and publisher would like to thank: The staff and residents of Badgworth Court (Mrs Tuck, Mrs Street, Mary Sherman–James, Hilda Penning, Harry Redman, Mr Pym); the Staff and Trustees of the Geffrye Museum, especially Vicky Woollard; Jeremy Farrell and David Taylor of the Nottingham Museum of Costume and Textiles; the staff of the Brewhouse Yard Museum, Nottingham; Suella Postles, Laura Spells, Jamil Hassan, Erin Knott, Laura Hopkin, Paul Watson, Charlotte Roberts, Ria Brookes, Sheena Roberts, and particular thanks to Gill Tanner.

Photographs by Maggie Murray except for: p 14 (bottom), 23 Barnaby's Picture Library; p 20 Mary Evans Picture Library; cover (inset), p 2 (bottom), 11 (top), 25 (bottom), 28 (top) The Hulton Picture Company; p 15 (top), 16 (top) The Illustrated London News Picture Library; p 14 (top) from the collection of Sheila Jackson; pp 8/9 The Museum of London; p 10 The Vestry House Museum (London Borough of Waltham Forest)